BELIEVE ME, I KNOW

WritersCorps
BOOKS

Edited by Valerie Chow Bush
Introduction by Jimmy Santiago Baca

Believe Me,

I Know

Poetry and Photography by WritersCorps Youth

*Writers*Corps

B O O K S

ISBN: 1-888048-08-5

**WritersCorps thanks the following for their contribution
to *Believe Me, I Know*:**

WritersCorps Selection Committee:
Valerie Chow Bush, Managing Editor
Janet Heller, WritersCorps Project Manager
Uchechi Kalu, WritersCorps Teacher
Asefa Subedar, WritersCorps Student
Jewelle Gomez, San Francisco Arts Commission

Mark Ong, Art Director

Sixth Street Photography Workshop:
S. René Jones
Billy Mitchell
Amanda Herman
Tom Ferentz, Artistic Director

Julie Felner, Copy Editor

2001-2002 WritersCorps Teachers: Cathy Arellano,
Uchechi Kalu, Michelle Matz, Danielle Montgomery,
Kimberley Nelson, Ishle Yi Park, Jime Salcedo-Malo, Chad
Sweeney, Gloria Yamato.

This book was printed by Somerset Printing in Burlingame,
California.

WritersCorps, a project of the San Francisco Arts
Commission, places writers in community settings to teach
creative writing to youth. The program is part of a national
alliance, with sites in the Bronx and Washington, D.C.,
whose shared vision is to transform and strengthen
individuals and communities through the written word.

WritersCorps gratefully acknowledges the support of the
Mayor's Department of Children, Youth and Their Families;
The Department of Juvenile Probation; The Walter and Elise
Haas Fund; The National Endowment for the Arts; the Lurie
Foundation; Borders Books and Music; The Gap, Inc.; and
individuals.

For more information, please call (415) 252-4655 or visit
www.writerscorps-sf.org.

CONTENTS

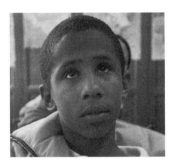

Chapter 2

Chapter 3

Chapter **5** Teachers' Writings

FOREWORD

Welcome to the eighth annual WritersCorps anthology, *Believe Me, I Know*. As the manager of WritersCorps since its inception eight years ago, I am particularly proud of the project's progress from an AmeriCorps federal pilot with a tenuous future to a national literary arts model. Every year, WritersCorps gives hundreds of San Francisco youth the opportunity to write, to be published, and to develop their strong voices. Dedicated teachers continue to be the backbone of the organization, inspiring youth, and working diligently to create a safe place for them to write and discover themselves in the process. In this past year, when our world has been deeply scarred by violence and hatred, WritersCorps' commitment to freedom of expression for youth remains as vital as ever.

This year's anthology is unique because, in addition to writing the poetry on these pages, WritersCorps youth took the photographs that grace the cover and interior of the book. Since January 2002, more than 400 youth have received training in photography from Sixth Street Photography Workshop, a San Francisco–based program that works with homeless adults. With professional photographers teaching them basic skills, WritersCorps students, ages six to 22, went on "Photo Walks" throughout San Francisco. For many, this was the first time they had ever used a 35mm camera or had a photo published. Some students who were reluctant to write blossomed as photographers. The students' photos, like their words, mirror their lives: The book pulses with faces of their friends and family, scenes of the busy city streets they travel every day, and images of the school playgrounds they know so well.

Believe Me, I Know, like the aperture of a camera, provides an opening—a momentary glimpse—into what it's like to be a young person living in San Francisco today. In their poems, the youth playfully tease their writing teachers, tell family secrets, share their dreams of love and peace, protest against institutions that oppress them, and reminisce about homelands they had to leave behind. Amidst their voices—their shouts, their whispers, their songs—there are those lasting moments when we see everything these young writers meant for us to see. Whether poetry is a wild animal, the smell of onions, or an ocean of words, poetry gives meaning to our lives. For this, I am sincerely grateful.

Janet Heller
Project Manager

INTRODUCTION

I have been teaching poetry to kids for years. I have seen what works in my students' eyes, in their gestures, in their genial sharing of opinions, laughter, and sadness. I have seen what works in the ways they open up to and teach each other.

Real learning is alive in the heart of every child. The poems in *Believe Me, I Know* attest to this truth and reaffirm my own belief that young people learn best when they believe they are being heard, that they are important, and that their experiences mean something.

As adults we tend to live day to day in sterile silence, never expressing what we really want to say. Most school experiences force children to shut down and keep quiet. The teachers of WritersCorps encourage just the opposite: In these poems, the youth sing out unabashedly. They refuse to play it safe, to take refuge from painful wounds. They boldly try to make sense of their world by confronting mistakes and exploring their feelings. They rebel against war, against racism, against intolerance and indifference.

These poems awaken a spirit of compassion and kindness in me. Some of them move me to tears, others to laughter—all move me to look at life in a different way.

Believe Me, I Know is a true testament to the power of writing and its ability to help us understand our world and fortify our place in it. In these pages, the voices of young people gather into a meeting of hearts opening to the world. As I read the work of these poets, I experienced anew the ceremony of being a child, of going on a field trip into the imagination. Their unpretentious poems advocate for an honesty that we adults all possessed at one time, an honesty that profoundly shaped our lives. Each poem in this collection is a road marker of every human being's journey into adulthood and our shifting place in the world.

The words on these pages move readers beyond skin colors, cultures, and languages by uniting us in a celebration of life's journey. Here and there, the students' poetic search glimmers with insights or darkens with hard lessons. But their writing always challenges us to confront our fears and loves. All of us, adults and youth alike, need writing that speaks to our hearts as real truths. That's exactly what the poems in *Believe Me, I Know* do: They allow readers to become vulnerable—open to hurt, open to love, open to experiencing the world in ways that permit us to grow.

Jimmy Santiago Baca
Jimmy Santiago Baca, winner of the Pushcart Prize and the American Book Award, is a poet and screenwriter. He is the author of *A Place to Stand*, a memoir.

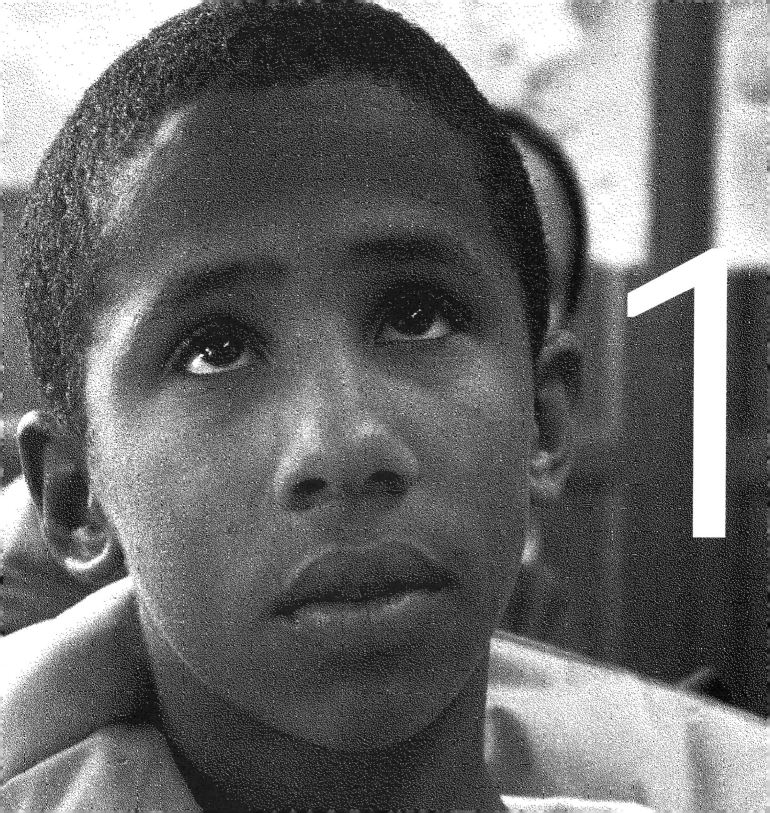

How to Sing

First, you have to open your mouth
so you can let out a song
that will make the birds jealous enough
to crack the sky.

Make the song so beautiful
angels cry.

Sing 'til church bells ring.
Sing from the heart.
Sing, baby, sing.

Dannesha Nash, 12
Everett Middle School

Everett Middle School

To Understand Me

To understand me
you have to know
how to do an ollie
on a skateboard.
You have to know
how my younger brother
bothers my friends
by thinking he's all that.
You have to understand
how the taco restaurant
at 16th and Mission makes tacos
with chile, onion, and cilantro.
You have to understand
my neighborhood,
how people say, "Good Morning"
when I walk to school.

Carlos Narvaez Duran, 12
Everett Middle School

Painting My Life

Inspired by Lisel Mueller's "Imaginary Paintings"

How I would paint sadness:

> seeing a little boy pass away,
> my mom crying
> because her sons died,
> making the rain come down
> from the sky.

How I would paint love:

> me and my boyfriend
> eating chocolate ice cream
> on a park bench.

How I would paint friendship:

> playing basketball
> in the park,
> going to the movies
> on Sunday night.

How I would paint my future:

> two good babies,
> a big house in New Mexico—
> the house is red,
> like birds,
> or fire.

Ashley Simms, 12
Everett Middle School

The Color of My Skin

The worst thing about being black
is always being seen
as a thief or troublemaker.

The worst thing about being black
is the police always watching me.

The worst thing about being black
is being forced to do things
you don't want to do but have to
to get by in the world.

The worst thing about being black
is people seeing me as a failure,
dropping out of school.

The worst thing about being black
is people seeing me as a person
who's going to end up in jail.

Michael Brown, 12
Everett Middle School

How to Be a Kid

Just to be a kid,
do silly things
like get stuck
in a chair.
Eat 700 pounds
of cotton candy.
Climb a tree
and eat a rotten apple.
Put dirty quarters
in your mouth.
Run around (scream).
Be stupid.
Just be a kid.

Erik Stern, 12
Everett Middle School

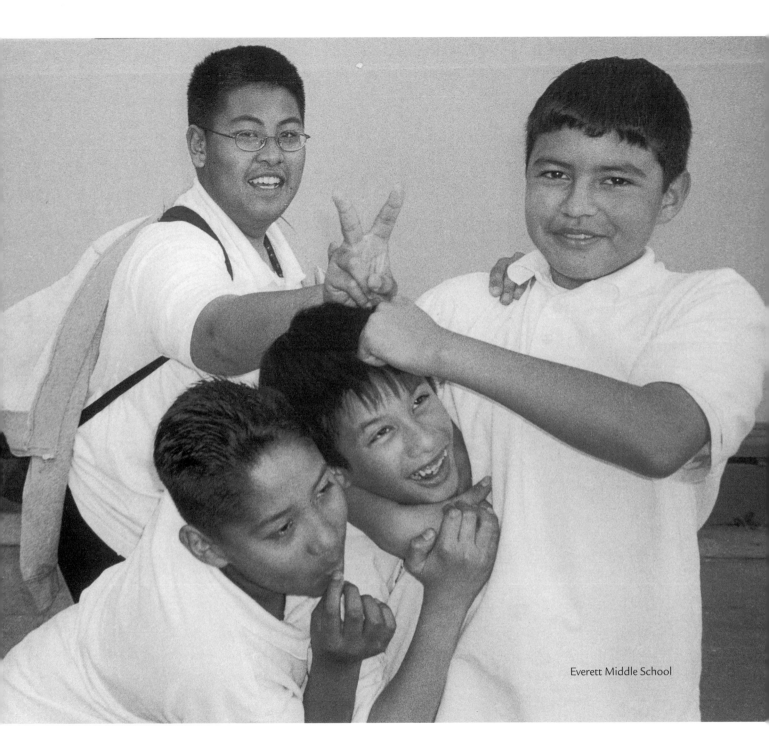

Everett Middle School

Hello

Hello to my neighbor,
the one across the street.

Hello to my bus driver,
the one that doesn't eat meat.

Hello to my cousin,
the one that goes to school with me.

Hello to my teacher,
the one that always loses her key.

Hello to the GASA staff,
who always help us with our work.

Hello to my mother,
the one that's going to have a baby
when I get home from school.

Chloe Underdue, 12
Girls After School Academy

Ten Years Old

I am a singer on the radio.
I am a player of dodgeball.
I am the newborn baby.
I am the butterflies in the park.
I am the midnight moon.
I am the president of the U.S.
I am inside the body of my goldfish.
I am the best student.
I am a superstar.
I am a child.
I am 10 years old.

Vanessa Tarantino, 10
Mission Girls

All About Miami

Miami is a fun place to visit.
There are cockroaches the size
of my hand.
There are sunny beaches and
cool swimming pools.
My brother lives in Miami.
I might visit him in the summer.
In Miami, there are trees
that look like coconut trees,
but they are not.

Thomas James Castrillo, 9
San Francisco Community School

Don't Judge Me

Don't judge me because I eat
Doritos. Don't judge me because
I eat burgers. Don't judge me
because I am small. Don't judge
me because I'm black. Don't
judge me because I ain't like you.
Don't judge me because I don't
look like you. Don't judge me
because I don't wear the same
thing as you. Don't judge me
because I don't do the same
things as you. Don't judge me
because I eat pizza.

Kashawn Johnson, 8
San Francisco Community School

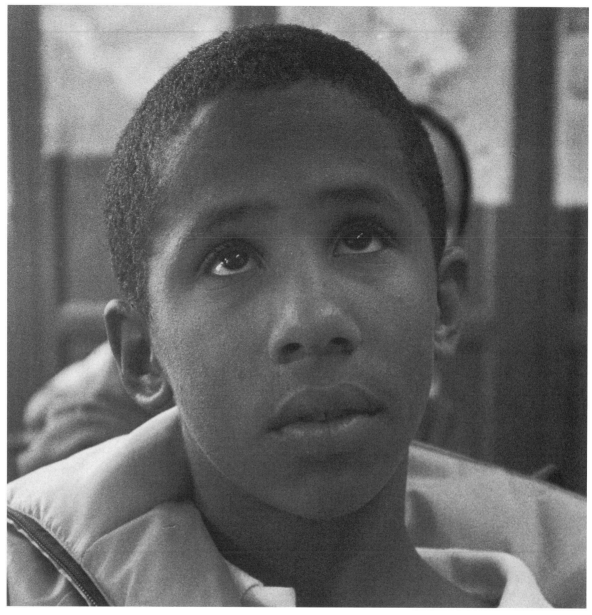

Everett Middle School

Questions

How come I'm small,
but in my family
I'm tall?

What if I die
at 60
and I come back
to life?

Suppose I was on that plane
and I stopped it
from crashing?

Nobody will listen
to what I have to say.

I should have helped my grandmother
when she was sick.

Why do I have to live
through this violence?
But I don't want to die.

Will I ever get a job
as a rapper
or a basketball player?

That's all I got to say
'cause I don't know
what to say.

Nico Wright, 12
Everett Middle School

Raven's Rhymes

One, two, three,
she looked at me.
Whee! Whee! I'm so happy!
Someone finally looked at me.

Four, five, six,
we built a house of sticks and
our clubhouse is made out of bricks.

Seven, eight, nine,
I like to make my poem rhyme
almost all the time.

Ten, eleven, twelve,
I would like to ride my bike with an elf.

Thirteen, fourteen, fifteen,
I saw a fly on the TV screen.

Raven Carter, 10
Girls After School Academy

Nappy Hair

My hair is nappy
and I sho am happy.
Well, I'm swinging my hair.
It's flying in the air!
Let me tell you, honey,
I love the way my hair is.
Knowing my hair,
I do care.
People think
long and short matter.
No! It don't
as long as you got some
on top of that beautiful, black
head of yours.
PEACE!

Angelica Pineda, 9
Girls After School Academy

When I Grow Up

I wish I would be a doctor,
cashier, or singer.
I would like first to be a singer,
then cashier and doctor.
I want to be a singer because
I could invent music.
I want to be a cashier
because I like to play
with the money
and I could put the food
in the bag.
I want to be a doctor
because it's fun.

Karina Ramirez, 11
Mission Girls

My Waist

My waist goes around
like a spinning top.
It can go round and round
and round and never stop.
It holds my upper body.
Every time we dance,
the waist stands out.

Jaleace Smith, 12
Girls After School Academy

Girls After School Academy

Brother Who

Brother who laughs
like thunder
and asks,
Who hears me?

Dan Campos, 12
Everett Middle School

Lost Gold

Once upon a time
I had some gold,
so I climbed a tree
to hide it.

A bird wanted my gold,
so he stole it
and flew to the moon.

Dillon Middlebrooks, 6
Mercy Services

Feet

Some feet are small
and some are big.
Some have bunions,
some have corns.
Some are black
and some are white.
You tell me what
your feet look like.

Darisha Moran, 12
Girls After School Academy

Flowers and Bees

When the flowers are thirsty and the leaves
are dry, merry little raindrops tumble
from the sky. All about they splatter
in their happy play, 'til the bright warm sunshine
chases them away.

I am yellow and I buzz. My tummy is
covered with fuzz. I make honey for you
and me. I am a honey bumblebee.

Fua Brown, 10
San Francisco Community School

The Tree

The tree of my mind
is happy and healthy when it is being loved
and cared for.
The roots suck up the love
to feed the leaves, trunk, and animals.

The birds in the tree are the voices inside,
which respond to my questions.
The owl is the tree's lookout while I sleep.

The monkeys in the tree
represent my craziness.
They swing from branch to branch,
screaming and playing different games.

The squirrel in my mind
collects food for the tree during winter.

When my mom hugs me, I am filled with joy,
and my mind sprouts flowers,
yellow and pink with green stems
to represent life and sunshine.

When my sister died
the tree became bare with nothing on it.

But when spring came again,
my tree grew new leaves.

Cierra Crowell, 9
Mercy Services

Newcomer High School

The Letter W

An upside-down M,
two sharp dog fangs,
two triangles,
a mother bird's beak giving her chicks
a worm.

William Tagade, 12
Everett Middle School

Erick

Erick's hair is black as a black bear.
Erick's eyes are dark as midnight.
Erick's ears are pears cut in half.
Erick's hands are rough.
Erick's heart is red.

Mio Montes, 9
San Francisco Community School

Philippines

In the Philippines I see people killing
pigs on a beach. I see a lot of traffic
and hear honking. I taste the food
that my grandma cooks.
I feel the heat from the sun.

Sean Picazo, 10
San Francisco Community School

How to Get a Girlfriend

First, you have to get to know her.
Then, get her a present.
Don't forget, girls like flowers.
Then tell her all about you
and then ask her,
"Do you want to be my girlfriend?"
If she says, "No," don't say nothing,
just walk away.
If she says, "Yes,"
don't act silly
because she may think you're stupid
and leave you for another boy.
Don't try to kiss her right away,
and don't talk bad to her.
If you follow my instructions,
you may just get one.

Lenin Salinas, 12
Everett Middle School

Anger

Anger lives in a lonely cave
where he even gets mad at the bats
for making noises while he is sleeping.

He wears a shawl around his shoulders,
sits on rocks, and spits in a bucket,
talking to himself because he's lonely.

He has black eyes, a fierce face,
red hands, and crooked yellow teeth,
with a mouth scrumped up into a grrrrr.

Anger does not have a wife
because he does not want to be responsible
for someone else,
so he scares them away.

Anger dreams of having friends,
not always being cruel and nasty,
but when hope flutters by his window
he closes the curtains.

Saman Minapara, 9
Mercy Services

Being a Child

The worst thing about being a child
is staying in a child's place,
never talking the way you want to,
always going to bed early
and getting up early,
never being able to say what you feel
in front of your parents,
and having to share a room.

Darnell Garrett, 12
Everett Middle School

We Are Sisters

I am the moon and my brother is the sun.
I am the god who rules the world.
I am the earth who's as wise as you.
I am the calendar that has all the dates of the year.
I am the light that shines.
I am the wrinkled hands that my grandma has from working.
I am the feather in the sky.
I am the tree that falls to give you oxygen.
I am the snow that's on top of the mountain.
I am the watch that works.
I am the cross around your neck.
I am the angel behind your back.

Alma Castro, 12
Elizabeth Hernandez, 10
Jessica Martinez, 12
Jessica Paz, 10
Vanessa Tarantino, 10
Mission Girls

People Come and Go

People come, people go,
but it doesn't really show.
Sometimes people have to go.

People think the world is
just all about being beautiful.

The world is about being
independent and working hard.
You're your own guard.

You really don't want
to be behind bars
for stealing cars.

Do something with your life.
Do you need some advice?
Do you need some ice
for your black eyes
from that fight?

You don't need to fight!
I thought you were
too beautiful to fight.

Remember, people come
and people go.

Kentoya Ginn, 11
Girls After School Academy

My Neighborhood

Ghettofabulous peeps hangin' around
a corner, sellin' weed in front of little kids.
People fighting here and der,
trash everywhere.
Taggin' on the streets,
gangs claimin' red or blue,
doin' things that ain't coo,
judgin' people by the way they look.
Other peeps think they all dat,
say they off the hook.
People bumpin' der music
in their car,
and all of a sudden someone died
because der was just a drive-by.
Peeps goin' da wrong way
instead of the right way.
It's so sad to see all da bad things
dat be happening at the place I live.
Some people so scared to pass by
to deliver somethin',
think when dey go to my neighborhood
it's the end of der lives.
But you know what?
Der life just started.
That's how dey do where I live.
Peeps might say this and dat
about my neighborhood,
but they just don't really know
what and how we do it in Frisko.

Catherine Anonuevo, 12
Everett Middle School

15th Street

My grandmother who
lives on 15th Street,
who cries when
she goes to church,
who hugs me good-night,
who is my right hand.

Armando Aguilar, 12
Everett Middle School

A Gift of Mine

I'm sending my sister a secret
to share with her
when she goes overseas.

I'm sending my father a cure
so he can breathe easy.

I'm sending my mother a heart,
since hers has been worn and torn.

I'm sending the love of my life
a letter to let him know
I'm home.

I'm sending my half-sister
a lot of love,
since my father left her lonely.

I'm sending my heart
to the edge of the earth.
I'm sending my soul to heaven,
to rest and be left in peace,
finally.

Evangelina Thomas, 12
Everett Middle School

Mercy Services

A Place

I come from a place
where cops is chasin' bums,
where trees are cut off,
where no bus runs by.
I come from a place
where da kids are playing,
where one gets along with the other.
I live in a city where it's pretty.
I live in a place so loud,
dat sounds like a roar of thunder,
where the kids are hungered.
I live in a place that is safe to me.
Where I come from is who I am.

Peehneka Long, 12
Everett Middle School

Sweet Mangoes

Philippines reminds me
of sinigang and lumpias,

sweet mangoes and my grandma's
good cooking,

my auntie who owns a candy store
and gave me gum,

Manila, the capital,
and my brother who took me to the mall.

Philippines reminds me of a young me.
I was skinny then.

Emmanuel Caramat, 12
Everett Middle School

Life

Right now I am sitting in the car
on Mission Street, parked in front of a Safeway
store, wondering what to write. A baby
is crying, a busy man is yelling at an old
woman to get out of the way, a little girl
wants a Monopoly game but her mom
won't buy it for her, a house on Shakespeare
Street is getting robbed, a bird is learning
how to fly, a ladybug is eating grass
at Dolores Park, a lion in Africa is getting
captured and sent to the zoo, a fire truck
is on the way to rescue people from the 9th floor
of an apartment building, a mother sacrifices
herself for her baby, a man is reading a newspaper
at a coffee shop.

Andrea Nguyen Thanh, 12
Everett Middle School

Nothin' but a Color

Peeps be thinkin' it's all about red or blue,
but one thing I gotta say is that ain't true.
Why do they give red and blue a bad name?
'Cause you know dem colors ain't nothin' but a thang.
Red is blood, which peeps lose all the time,
blue is the feeling families be havin' when they say,
Why couldn't it have been somebody else's child
instead of mine?
Lives taken,
families shaken,
why do all these peeps gotta be fakin'?
It's all about guns and knives
but they use that as an excuse to hide what's inside.
What they put themselves through ain't nothin'
compared to what they really could do!
Once they 'bout to get jumped
they see nobody carin',
leavin' they dead bodies at a city dump.
Lost lives,
unheard cries,
tryin' to find a way out,
not wantin' the gang to be all they're about.
Drugs,
wannabe thugs,
not having to keep lookin' over your shoulder.
You're in an alley, dying, it's getting colder.
Drug addicts,
cocaine fanatics,
ain't got no money can't do without it.

Lookin' back on the lives they would've had,
gotta worry if their family is safe,
mom or dad tweakin' off dope.
Damn! Ain't got nothin' to smoke.
Expectin' a white light
but instead gettin' into a fight.
Gunshots,
your life flashing before your eyes.
No, no! you hear your mom's cries.
You're thinking it's just begun,
but then you realize,
Oh no,
it's over,
it's done.

Vanessa Martinez, 12
Everett Middle School

Hope

Hope lives in the middle
of a rainforest
where no man has ever been.
His house is made of green and red
gummy worms and popcorn
with blue curly fries for a bed.

Hope wears a black sweatshirt, jeans,
and a red hat with an "H" on it.

His eyes are like stars in the dark,
and his mouth
is half a smile.

Miguel Haro, 12
Mercy Services

To Be a Girl

To be a real girl
you have to know
how to handle yourself.
To be a girl
you have to know
how to treat others
and respect yourself.
To be a girl
you have to know
what's life
and how to live life.
Also, you have to know
the bad from the right.
And don't ever let anyone
touch your body
if you don't want them to.

Mariela Castillo, 11
Mission Girls

To Wonder

The worst thing
about being a child
is having no mother,
to only have a father,
to never feel her touch,
never take a single look
at her again,
to always wonder where she is,
what she's doing,
what she's feeling.
To always wonder.

Alfredo Diaz, 12
Everett Middle School

My Grandpa and Me

My grandpa who
used to help me read,
who thinks about his black stallion
in Mexico,
who brings me medicine
when I'm sick,
who loves to race his horse,
who helps my sister,
who cries when I say good-bye,
who sits on the porch
and talks with his friends
about his cornfields,
who calls me
My Little Drop of Rain.

Danny Garcia, 12
Everett Middle School

Girls After School Academy

I Want to Send

a plastic frog to Mr. Zapien
because he likes 'em.

a better school to Ms. Hernandez
because she needs one really bad.

a garden to my grandma
because she loves plants.

color pencils
and everything an artist needs
to my uncles
so they'll paint this world peaceful.

more money to El Salvador
so that there won't be more sadness.

my neighbors happiness
because their dog died two years ago.

Michelle a large big room
so that she could teach us
in a private room just for her.

a letter to myself
so that I could remember
when I was a child.

Carlos Cartagena, 12
Everett Middle School

Bravery

There is a bear
inside of me.
It is my anger and bravery.
It is my soul.

I love you so much,
little bear.

Sara Aylward-Brown, 7
Mercy Services

Odes

Ode to Ishle

She looks like the lady who lives downstairs,
she sounds like birds singing when she talks,
she feels like a lotus petal, so creamy and soft,
she smells like perfume,
she laughs like a hyena.

Ode to Jime

He looks like a robot,
he sounds like the Backstreet Boys,
he feels like a lion,
he smells like my dad,
he walks like an alien from outer space.

Karman Zhu, 9
San Francisco Community School

Haiku

poor old rotting flower
there is nothing to do with
you but to compost

Ivan Cheng, 9
San Francisco Community School

Gloria

I can see Gloria.
She has beautiful dreads.
She has on a coat that
has a soft cotton texture
that makes her look
even stronger than she is.
She's a very nice lady.
You should get to know her
because she knows what to do
to get you in shape.
You wouldn't want
to get on her bad side
because no more fun for you.

Ebony Branner, 11
Girls After School Academy

To the People That I Love

I'm sending my grandma beautiful roses.
As her life dies she will dream
with her roses.

I'm sending my mom a ring.
She will be sure of my father's love.

I'm sending my brother letters.
He will read them and remember
a good sister.

I'm sending Jimmy
a few packs of cigarettes.
He will smoke them faster
as he rides away in his car,
drunk.

I'm sending lipsticks to my cousin.
She will use them
to keep her beautiful face.

I'm sending my father my car.
He is a good mechanic and will repair it
for me.

I'm sending my niece a dog.
She will take care of him
and the dog will help her cross streets.

I'm sending my friend
a good friendship.
She will be happy to know
that she has a truthful friend.

Ivette Perez, 12
Everett Middle School

My Name

My name is blue in the sky
with white cloud polka dots.

My name is ginger, sweet as maple syrup,
with a touch of brown skin.

But call me angel
like the person I should be,
protecting my family.

Call me tornado
sweeping my once wet tears,
now dry memories.

Call me African American beauty
with class and excellence.

But my real name,
my true name,
is Dionne,
the person inside of me.

Dionne Spencer, 13
Everett Middle School

The World Is Open

Being young in San Francisco is the greatest.
Your life is full of friends and fun.
Your world is open to different cultures,
many faces of joy, sadness, and excitement.

In San Francisco you have many places
to see, feel, and hear.
Going down the street you see people
getting along with each other.
Another time, maybe, they are not getting along,
hating, dissing, and killing each other,
and not just with guns, but with drugs and words.

Being young in San Francisco is good,
as long as you are careful
and know who your friends are.

Jose Delgadillo, 14
Everett Middle School

Everett Middle School

Uttarayan, Festival of the Kites
Ahmadabad, India

In the blink of an eye
wingless birds overpower the skies,
beautiful combinations of colors
arise in the thousands of kites
that soar the low heaven.

On this day winter is over and summer has begun.
The sun continues its drift toward the highest throne.
All of India's men, women, and children stand upon their roofs,
Muslim beside Hindu, Christian beside Sikh,
connecting their minds to the red and white
dragonflies darting in sharp angles above.

Countless numbers of heads look up all day,
praising the sun
for releasing its warmth upon their faces.

Every string is painted with tiny glass shards
so that the paths might cross in playful battle,
cutting the strings and releasing the kites to the wind.
Street children run like wild beasts
to catch the fallen kites and sell them for one rupee.

The innocent pleasure of this festival
spells its name across the faces of rickshaw drivers,
factory workers, and doctors,
each laughs and smiles open-mindedly,
knowing there is no work today or tomorrow.

As the day comes to an end, pollution begins to rise
in clouds of blooming flowers, a dull finishing of red.
The sun slowly drowns into the ocean
in sheets of blue flame.

Shahid Minapara, 14
Mercy Services

Call Me

My real identity is in the wings
of a bird soaring on a natural high,
just to fly, just to fly.
My secret name is African-French-Indian-American,
the roots of an enchanting queen,
intelligent in many ways with happiness and solitude.

I am the rolling hills of green pain
that haunt my sorrowful dreams,
a weeping willow in the company of the dead.

Call me rainy harmony, Cleopatra,
chocolate and caramel melting in your mouth.

Call me by my many names.
Call me what I am.
Call me sorrow!

Christina Sherrills, 13
Everett Middle School

Coconut Milk

Sunset turns the blue sky
into red, purple, and orange.
Small, warm breezes lift
the hair out of your face.
Palm trees cover your surroundings.
You just sit in your chair
looking into the sun and listening
to the water splash against the sand.

A coconut falls and breaks open.

You see the white inside, the sparkling milk.
You think of the white meat before the coconut opened.
It was caged in the coconut darkness
with the memory of its ancestors,
used to manufacture grease
for our people's hair.

One coconut brother was sold
to an old woman.
She drinks its milk now
with such a refreshing feeling,
then closes her eyes and wishes
to be with you
on that beach,
thinking and thinking.

Rigoberto Canchola, 13
Everett Middle School

Newcomer High School

No Friends

Anger
lives in an abandoned house
on the other side of town.

He wears a leather jacket
with spikes at the shoulders,
torn-up blue jeans,
and a macho chain.

Anger doesn't have any friends
because he bullies everyone.
His enemy is happiness.

Francisco Quevedo, 13
Everett Middle School

Growing Up in San Francisco

I.
What a sweet little flower,
confident
to grow bigger.
Focused on spreading her arms
against all the pressure
causing her to fail.

Hold on, little flower.

II.
When they tell you about the city,
it's from an adult point of view.
They brag about all the great things
not allowed for teen eyes to see.

Growing up in the city,
I feel as if I'm trapped in a cage:
too young to go out,
but too old to play double Dutch.

Sabina Hatipovic, 13
Everett Middle School

The Sweater

A sweater washed away by the rain
settled near a front porch
where an old woman lived.

When the sun rose
the woman came out and found the sweater
and took it inside.

She said to herself
that the sweater had sheltered other people
from the harsh weather of the past,
so she washed and fixed it.

The sweater came from the wool
of a sheep.
It warmed the sheep, she thought, and people too,
and many journeys carried the sweater to her.
Now the old sweater was ready
for another journey.

Jorge Pacheco, 13
Everett Middle School

Sleepwalking

I wander through the rooms of my dream.

There is a jail.
A pale girl sits in the corner,
stroking her doll's hair.

The next room is made of glass,
and I can see myself
in all six directions.

The next room has trees and bushes.
Rain falls from the ceiling and grass pokes up,
beetles running across the floor.

In the last room I find myself
on my deathbed.

Joseph Daniel, 13
Everett Middle School

Guatemala

I am from Todos Santos,
a little town of mud houses
and rock streets
in the mountains
where it is difficult to drive.

Saturdays people come from other towns
to the market
where you can find many things.
Everyone speaks Mam,
a Mayan language,
and dresses in Mayan clothing.

First day of November we have a celebration.
The horses run
and people dance in the streets,
the Mayan people of Guatemala dance.

Wilson Jimenez, 14
Everett Middle School

Sleep

The windows are blue.
The colorful moonlight
shines on the blue glass,
and you can see through the doors.

The dreams are hats
hung
on
the
wall.

Dexter Ganaden, 13
Everett Middle School

First Love

I was in the third grade,
yet so afraid.
It was a girl with the beauty of a dove.
She was like a breeze on a hot day.
When she talked, I hung on her every word.
Just to know that I would
see her every day made me wake up
early to see her face.
I was only in the third grade, yet so afraid.
I never knew what to say to convince
her I'd been walking on air
since I met her.
I'd never felt this way.
I was in the third grade,
yet so afraid.
I wished she could breathe out
so I could breathe her in.

Justin Gordon, 15
International Studies Academy High School

International Studies Academy High School

House of Dreams

In the house of dreams
there are pictures on the wall
that smile at me
when I wake up in the morning.

Through the ceiling
I can communicate
with my dead family members.

Sometimes my grandmother
sits on the stairs
drinking her coffee
the way she used to do.

The fireplace flames up
with memories of my life,
a magical TV of dreams.

The cabinets open
if I ask them to,
and birds are free to fly
all about the house.

Reygen Pardilla, 13
Everett Middle School

On My Block

Weekends in Hunter's Point
is always hot with police
messing with you,
jacking you for no reason.
Mostly they're crooked,
like to slip things into your pockets,
beat you
when they catch you doing something.

Things I hear at night are crazy,
gunshots and fights,
somebody always getting killed.

Most of the time it isn't too bright
to walk around in Hunter's Point,
so I just stay on the block.

Jermayne Edwards, 14
Everett Middle School

School Uniform

I don't like the school uniform
because it's white and black.
When I see my school,
it looks like a movie from the 1930s.

When I look at other schools,
all the girls have different dresses
of many colors,
like a garden of flowers,
roses.

My school looks like an old garden
of sad flowers,
roses without life.

Lemny Hernandez, 14
Everett Middle School

The Crossing

There is an old Chinese man
dressed in blue
with a big shade hat.
He stands barefoot on a boat,
pushing the boat with a bamboo pole
across the green water
toward a forested mountain.

At the foot of the mountain
are two houses
surrounded by trees
in the early light.

Lucia Zavala, 14
Everett Middle School

Mission High School

Nothing Feels Right

I need to write about
how nothing feels right, everything feels wrong.
How my grades are going down
and everything else with it.
How the work is too much
for me to handle.
How parents complain, "It's not good enough,"
but what they don't know is that
that's the best I can do.
How siblings talk too much and get you in trouble,
you just want to bury them alive,
but in your heart you know you love them.
How someone you love has gone away for a while.
You know they'll be back,
but you can't help but cry.
How you want to cry,
but you don't want anyone to think something is wrong,
so you hide behind a smile,
but inside you know you're sad.
I need to write about all this,
so I can get it off of my chest.

Jenna Muya, 15
International Studies Academy High School

Everything Is Alive

The grocery store feels regretful
because he ate candy apples,
chocolate bars, and ice cream,
and his stomach is going to explode.

The beach is depressed because she hasn't
had a bath for so long.
Alcatraz feels ill after all the stormy weather
wet his head and soaked his coat.

The jewelry store feels rich
wearing gold on her fingers and arms.
The fire truck is getting nervous
because he doesn't want to get burned.

The bridge is exhausted from transporting
people on its back from city to city.
And the flowers are dying of thirst,
for not one drop has slipped down their throats.

Desiree Gomez, 13
Everett Middle School

The Real Me

I'm not the prisoner, but the officer.
I'm not the mouse, but the snake.
I'm not the world, but the universe.
I don't follow it, I lead it,
and I learn it, bit by bit.

Don't see me as an "F," but as an "A"
embossed on a white sheet.
Don't see me as a lie in a liar's mind,
but as the truth in all who are kind.
Talk to me, I'm not ignorant.
I'm Peruvian, not an "Immigrant."

Don't see me as dumb, see me as wise.
Come follow me into the world of paradise.

Joyce Bonilla, 13
Everett Middle School

Possible

Positive people get far in life. They
Oh, so rarely
See the dark gray
Skies of
Impossible
Blue waters
Locked in dark
Electric skies of negative light.

Jennifer Johnson, 15
San Francisco Public Library, Main Branch

Georgia Reminds Me

Hot summer days,
all the trouble we'd get into
for stealing peaches off people's trees,
old folk sitting on the porch,
rocking back and forth,
gossiping about young folk
thinking they're in love.
Georgia reminds me
of when we had no milk
and had cereal with water.

Ephesia McClure, 14
Everett Middle School

Lil Mama

Short, loud, loving, crazy,
she's a dancer.
Talks too much shit,
don't know what she's saying
half the time.
Some people call her Lil Mama.
That's her name.
They call her Ghetto Girl.
Don't know how to fight,
but knows how to protect herself.
She's very smart,
but don't use her smartness.
There she goes, Lil Mama.
She like you or she don't.

Vanessa Lima, 13
Mission Girls

Starleena

Striving for more.
To look for my
Ambition, not to
Rely on
Love. My
Eagerness, trying to
Enjoy life by
Nature, nature
Awaits me.

Starleena Hernandez, 13
San Francisco Public Library, Main Branch

Sadness

Sadness is like
a dull knife
you can't cut with.

Veronica Barrios, 12
Everett Middle School

The Healing

With my healing hands I will cure
every disease in the world,
so people won't have to worry.

With my healing hands I will erase
racism, prejudice, and sexism,
turn them into three more stars
in the sky.

Susana Sandoval, 13
Everett Middle School

Mission Girls

Loud Poem

This poem has attitude.
This poem mugs people all day.
When this poem don't like people, she lets them know.
This poem gets smart with teachers.
When this poem gets mad, everybody knows.
As Luda says, "Throw dem bows."
This poem kicks and screams and gets very loud.
When people say this poem should be ashamed, she says,
"No! I'm proud."

Morgan Walton, 15
International Studies Academy High School

Today Ain't All That

I put on 2 left shoes
kids at school stepped on me
walked out of the house with no $
my hair not done
and all that I could think was
Man, no Juicy Fruit gum.
Was late 2 homeroom
skipped detention
almost got sent home for cursing out
my science teacher
missed my good show
('cause my grandma fussin' & cussin')
went 2 bed early without dinner.
Man, where's my Juicy Fruit gum?

Deloris Vaughn, 13
Everett Middle School

My Dreams

When I was little, I wanted to be a doctor,
but I heard being a doctor is too difficult.
I have to study hard and for a long time,
and I just think I can't do that.
I'm scared, I'm scared to fail.

And now I love to do poems and calligraphy.
I want to be a professional poet and also a beautiful calligrapher.
I know that I have to take art,
but I'm scared, I'm scared to fail.
Because I heard it's too difficult and expensive to learn art.

I want to have a good boyfriend who will be my husband,
but I'm scared, scared if he is just a liar.

Because I'm not beautiful.
I want to be brave.
But I'm scared, scared people will laugh at me.

I hate to be like this.
I'm sick.
I want to be free,
free from this fear.
But how?
I don't know.

Irene Parma, 15
Newcomer High School

Insane

I'm incarcerated!
Caged like a bird.
When will I find my freedom?
When will I be able to tell you what I truly feel?
Now is the time.
Now is the time to break those bars.
They can't hold me anymore.
You thought you had me, didn't you?
You thought I wouldn't escape this hellhole.
You thought your contraption was too Einsteinish for me.
Well, guess what?
I am free!
Free from all the pain and lies.

Lafayette Reed, 13
San Francisco Community School

My Country

I'm in the United States
missing the parties
and the food,
the rich carapulcra and the masamorra,
all kinds of music too,
the tranx, la salsa, and cumbia.
I miss the delicious beverages
of my country,
la chicha, el pisco sour, and the most delicious, la cristal.
I miss the big mountains and the ruins,
the ruins of Machu Picchu.

Daniel Lau, 15
Newcomer High School

Mission Girls

How Poetry Feels

To wake up
on a bright, Saturday morning
with the smell of pancakes,
the day is like a wild animal.
You don't know what comes next.

Poetry is your bird.
The mind is free, and your pencil is alive.
Your thoughts pour
into the ocean of words.

Poetry feels like putting words
on paper with secret meanings
only you can understand.
When people read your poems
they give the words new meanings.

A poem is born
and passed around
to give light to others.

Angela Anderson, 13
Everett Middle School

Mami

Mami who tells me
to be good with my brother,
who gives love
to my brother and me,
whose face is made of cream,
who is an angel,
who cooks my favorite chicken soup.
Who is too sad,
see her cry.
Who asks me in Spanish,
Quién es el corazóncito adentro del mio?
and tells me in Mayan,
What a sincere heart you have.
Who sometimes makes me feel bad
when she yells at me
when I hit my brother.
Mami, whose eyes are like a chocolate bar,
who used to laugh when I said jokes.
Mami who is my only hope
for my future.
My heart is asking,
Did you love your Mami?
And then I ask myself,
Who else loves Mami?

Charly Uc, 13
Everett Middle School

The Projects

The projects are filled with drugs and thugs,
feels like being stuck in a black box
with an angry green fox, and guns hot
after a shot.

A stripped car feels naked with no tires,
the ground dirty with diapers and blood,
stained from a fight two months ago.
A drunk man shatters a bottle of 211,
and money is sad because you don't have a job,
standing on the corner selling rocks.

The air is wheezing from all the weed smoke.
After a dogfight, the cold, dead
body of a dog lying with no soul.

The building's body aches
from the loud music
and people staying out all night.

Tazia Payne, 13
Everett Middle School

Under Fire

Back in the day
there weren't so many problems,
no war, no guns.

Now we destroy:
It's all we do,
all we're good at.

Back in the day
there were no bombs, no explosions,
only simple talk of finding a home.

Now we have homes
and we fight over them
instead of sharing.

Back in the day
life was better
than these days under fire.

Marco Moon, 15
Mercy Services

What I've Seen

I need to write about
all the hatred in this world,
all the racist people,
all the wars, the fights, the arguments.
I've seen too many people in pain,
like a bird without its nest
trying to find a home.
I've seen little girls
cry in their moms' arms,
making it harder for their mothers
to go on
because they don't want
to see their daughters in pain—
to see them crying.
I've seen it,
and I know how it is,
because I was one
of those little girls.

Zelkja Lazic, 15
International Studies Academy High School

International Studies Academy High School

Mary

Motivated to change what's not right.
Angry at people who judge me too quickly.
Ready to express my real self.
Yes, I do want to be your friend.

Mary Brutto, 14
San Francisco Public Library, Main Branch

My Momma

My momma told me God don't like ugly
don't talk about it, be about it
get in where you fit in or be without it
and you are never too old to get a whippin'
and if you too hot, get yo ass out of the kitchen.

Antonio Gilton, 15
International Studies Academy High School

Mi Pueblo

Mi pueblo es un anillo
redeado de perlas y diamantes.
Es muy chico pero muy lindo.
Gente viene y gente va,
pero mi pueblo nunca cambiará.

Estoy orgullosa de mi pueblo
porque allí nací y crecí.
No importa donde esté
ni donde iré,
mi pueblo siempre estará allí
representándome a mí.

My Town

My town is a ring
encircled by pearls and diamonds.
It's small, but very lovely.
People come and go,
but my town will never change.

I am proud of the town
where I was born and raised.
It doesn't matter where I am
or where I will go,
my town will always be there
representing me.

Maria Garcia, 13
Everett Middle School

Wolf

I have a wolf who has silver skin.
I have a wolf who is freedom.
I have a wolf who has yellow eyes, the eyes
of the predator.
I have a wolf who is the fighter for freedom
and independence.
I have a wolf who has a very high spirit.
I have a wolf who is very brave and who has hot blood.
I have a wolf who is very kind but, at the same time,
he is very strong.
I have a wolf who cannot reconcile with spirit jails,
who needs all spirits of the forests and all powers of the wind,
the might of the ocean, and the handsome beauty of the fire.

Alexsey Shrayber, 14
Newcomer High School

Morning Glory

Soft leaves run
up and down the gate
leading to the
blue-violet blossom.

M'kia McCright, 13
YWCA, Western Addition

Hummingbirds

A cloud dreamily watched
angry helicopters
zoom by with crazy speed.

The ocean was ticklish
with fish and sea creatures
moving like a motor in her stomach.

The jail felt guilty
while humans used his teeth
for bars.

The pond
was lovestruck by the moon
looking down on him every night.

The flowers felt playful
under the touch
of the hummingbirds.

Huu Viet Chau, 14
Everett Middle School

My Auntie Miguelina

Auntie Miguelina who danced
every time, at a party or alone,
who took care of Riqui,
a little bird,
who walked all the time
in her little garden
with all kinds of roses
and plants,
who called to me, *Mari,*
who taught me how to dance,
who in the night
stayed in a black window
and looked at cars pass,
who said to me,
Vamos a meter los borregos, Mari?
who played with my cousins and me
on Sundays in the yard
with bottles of water,
who said to me every time,

Be good with your mother,
help your mother,
who gave me the advice,
Don't lose your dreams,
who told me,
Study, Mari, you need to be
someone in life,
you are very intelligent.
Auntie Miguelina,
whose place no one
is going to take.

Maritza Salinas, 13
Everett Middle School

Skateboarding

Riding down the street
with the wind pressing against my skin,
trying to accomplish the trick.
Defect in my mind, no.
Success, yes.
I finally got it,
the move I want to do day and night.
I love this place where the wind is always cool,
where the sun is always shining
in front of my house.

Joshua Hellpap, 13
San Francisco Community School

A Cloud

A cloud
in a sky of neighbor clouds.
It's not lonely,
it has all these poofy friends
who make good pillows to cry on.

They all float around together,
forming shapes,
collecting water to shower on the ground below,
deciding what the weather will be.
After all, they are clouds.
They have fun together,
they always do.
They float together in the sky.
They share.
It has quite a bit of room also.

The people below point and think,
"Wouldn't it be great to be a cloud?"
The clouds chuckle and move on,
they move on, always moving.
That's why a cloud has so many friends.

Grace Harpster, 13
San Francisco Community School

Those Days

Running
jumping
that's what I did.
Childhood fights
pulling girls' hair.
Those were the days.

Nutrition, uh,
eating nothing but junk food—
Man! I got in trouble for those dentist bills.
Going to the park
going on field trips.
I miss that.

Having a crush on girls
they were hecka old.
Recess
lunchtime.
I miss those.
Having nothing to worry about.
Those were the days.

No grades
no stress.
Falling
getting scarred up
bleeding.
None of it hurt
but the sight of blood
made me cry.
Wish I could get those days back.

Marcus Grogans, 15
International Studies Academy High School

When Will It End?

You may say they deserve it,
but do they really?
When will it end?
They bomb us,
we bomb them,
that's no help to the world peace we are trying to reach.

Their dying doesn't make those who died come back.
It is all about revenge.
We want them to feel the pain we feel,
the grief we feel,
the anger we feel.
But does that take us closer to world peace?
No.

Suzy Chen, 13
San Francisco Community School

My Tio

My tio used to love me
and still does.
My tio took care of me,
fed me like his child,
made my bottle,
picked me up from daycare,
took me to feed the bums under the freeway.
My tio made me run
for the bus,
crashed his truck
into a pole.
My tio got kicked out of his house.
The night he got to my house,
he made me trip and bump my head
on a chair.
My tio killed
all my cats
and slept like a bear.
The one and only tio.
He said,
I love you,
and said,
I'll be back to see you.
My tio, the one I will probably never see again,
only in my head and pictures.
That's the one-in-a-million tio.
That's the tio I love.

Veronica Courtade, 13
Everett Middle School

Whenever My Name Is Mispronounced

Whenever my name is mispronounced,
I want to sound my name to his ears,
until he puts his hands on his ears,
until he jumps and runs away fast,
until he falls down on the road,
until he says my name the right way.

Whenever my name is mispronounced,
I want to take him to the forest,
change him into a fish,
put it in a whale's mouth,
change him into an egg,
cook it, eat it,
change him into a rock,
throw it to the river,
until he says my name the right way.

Jing Yan Liu, 15
Newcomer High School

Everett Middle School

Anything

Poetry is the story of the soul
vivid pictures
that pulse through our minds.

Pictures of the night sky
our fears
our living dreams.

The poetry
of beautiful things
dreadful things
anything.

Janudine (Tom) Tran, 13
Everett Middle School

Safety Issues

Wanting to shut my TV off,
throwing my radio across the room.
It sounds like the blast of the Twin Towers,
a thousand times softer.
Trying to calm the voices in my head.
It's aching when you can't find 5,000 dead.
They say they want stretchers.
For what? Body parts and heads?
Races, colors, faces, dreams, unbelievable.
The images coming through my TV screen
of one after the other
Twin Towers falling to the streets.
Turned off my TV, wanting to get away.
It's all I can read: newspaper after newspaper,
article after article, picture after picture.
Things are going cold in me.
Don't stop our normal lives, they say.
But we can't get regular programmin' on MTV.
They say, *Go back to work,*
nothing to worry about.
I think everyone is standing still,
waiting for a pin to drop,
or the next plane to crash, the next bomb to go off.
Such a fast-paced world, never stopping.
Nothing's normal, never has been.
Now we're just not moving at all.

Safety. Safety has never changed for me.
My security, my government, senators, congress
are my family, loved ones, close friends—the love I have for another
and the love they show me.
Forget the President, PoPos, or the IRS.
They don't know me.
Never done anything for me but bombed other places,
slammed people's faces into car doors,
handcuffed innocent people, and
taken down drug lords for the millions of cash that they got.
Seeing crying faces, hearing sirens, revving engines,
frantic people running.
I run to my family, my mother and father,
and feel safe.

Cynthia A., 17
The Center for Young Women's Development

You Say

"Immigrant," you say.
But I was here first,
so, who's really the immigrant?
You act like you're better than me,
but really we're the same.
The only thing that makes us different
is the color of our skin.
So, do you still dare call me immigrant?
If you do, then
just think back to who
was here first.

Olivia Marquez, 17
Mission High School

Chinese Dragon

There is a huge dragon in the faraway East,
I am looking for it everywhere.

"Have you seen the dragon?"
I ask the historian.
But he just knows a dragon whose age is 5,000 years,
experienced many dynasties—rose and fell,
who is the origin of the world civilization.

"Have you seen the dragon?"
I ask the chef.
But he just knows a dragon whose eyes are dumplings,
whose beard is noodles and the horns are spring rolls,
whose thousands of scales are barbecued pork.

"Have you seen the dragon?"
I ask the doctor and geographer.
But they just know a dragon whose artery
is the Yangtze River and the vein is the Yellow River,
whose heart is named Beijing and the head is Tibet,
whose body is the wriggling Great Wall.

"Have you seen the dragon?"
I ask my father and mother.
They tell me that dragon is a large imaginary animal with enormous power.
The truth is, there is no dragon in the real world,
but I believe firmly that there must be a red dragon in my heart,
whose name is China,
my dearest homeland.

Coco Guo, 16
Newcomer High School

Hear My Name

Whenever my name
is mispronounced,
I want to take myself
back to China,
hear the correct sound, *Zhi Hong.*
Zhi is like
when you just put the egg
into the hot oil;
Hong is like
when the big dogs see a stranger
come to them.

Zhi Hong Lin, 16
Newcomer High School

Vero Who?

I am a person,
paint and painful,
color and art.
I am something that is broken,
which annoys the hell out of people.
I am small, a mouse, a rat, a cat.
Orange juice,
and November skies,
dots that my nephews easily scatter
throughout a thousand and one pages.
Black replaceable ink,
a sketch of an unfinished masterpiece,
forever reaching
for something impossible.
A lion's prey,
slick but scared.
I am a proud blend of blue and white
with yellow.
I am unpronounceable words.
I am cocoa, milk,
sugar, and cinnamon.
I am what I am.

Veronica Castro, 17
Loco Bloco

Listen

Don't tolerate abuse of any kind:
verbal, physical, mental—
they'll all fuck up your mind.
Baby girl,
listen to this:
Don't ever think that shit is cool
just because you got him pissed.
When he tells you that he loves you
and that he'll never do it again,
don't listen.
Bring the relationship to an end.
Know and believe that you are a precious jewel.
Don't let that clown play you for a fool.
Hold your head up, go for what's best.
Then let God do the rest.
Don't ever let a man tell you that you're not worth shit.
Remember:
NO ONE can love you like you can.

Tiffany Latrice Trammell, 17
The Center for Young Women's Development

Two Worlds

I am a teenage girl
who was once portrayed by the virtue of innocence.
Before my eyes brought into my brain
clouds of contamination,
pot becoming the center of teenagers' attention,
you might not think so, but
there's something wrong with my generation's true obsession.

I am a wise girl
who was brought up in that quarter of the city
where drug dealing flows in, often continuously,
because of the social, legal, and economic pressures,
and for some reason, the majority are minorities.

I am a gay girl,
which is a secret that I rarely expose,
but those whom I really want to tell I can't inform.
Live a double life is what I do.
In one,
I may be in love with a girl,
but in the other,
I listen to how homosexuality is a major sin of this world.

Anonymous, 16
International Studies Academy High School

San Francisco Community School

My Brother

My brother who is a bamboo pole,
sometimes I am jealous of him.
He always eats too much, but he's never fat.
Also, his skin is better than mine.

Sometimes I hate him.
His smile is very fake, but
when he laughs it is a loudspeaker.
He is shy, so when he has some questions,
he always asks me to ask other people.
So, many people think that I am older than him.
"No! I am his younger sister!" That's what I always say.
When we were young, we often fought,
and I always got hurt and I was angry. Now,
I've grown up. We never fight, but
we always dispute.

Sometimes I love him so much, but
I've never told him.
He's kind to me.
I like his fried rice, which is delicious.
Maybe one day, I will say to him,
"I love you, my brother! My only one."

Zhi Min Lin, 16
Newcomer High School

Rare Rose

I am a rare blue rose,
damn near one-of-a-kind,
short with thick stems,
with velvet petals opening to the light.
I stand out in a dozen that all look alike,
the way I stand tall
in the roar of sunlight,
waiting for the right person
to pick me out and say
I am the finest.
Dress me in the finest vase
with pure clear water.
Sit me on top of the finest linen
and show me that in life I matter.

DeAngela Barnett, 16
International Studies Academy High School

New Year's Eve

I like New Year's Eve.
Time: 12:00 a.m., midnight,
wonderful see firework really beautiful.
I feel so good happy for me
because this is New Year's Eve.

Taste none one anyone...but good
food delicious Filipino wonderful.

I look at fireworks,
really pretty pop and loud.

When start pop firework then finish,
I smell like a powder I don't know,
look like smells.

Alexa Mendoza, 16
English Literacy, Deaf Education Program
International Studies Academy High School

My Horses

I had horses who were hungry at night.
I had horses whose skin reflected the light.
I had horses who kicked the stall when they needed food.
I had horses who ran very fast.
I had horses who had black blown skin.
I had horses who were very thin.
I had horses who liked to take a shower.
I had horses who liked to sit in the Land Rover.
I had horses who swam with the sharks.
I had horses who stood in the harsh wind.

Rattaphol Yuvananggoon, 16
Newcomer High School

Just Plain Melvin

My name is boring, like a dark and wet winter day.
My name smells, like ocean water on a dry summer day.
My name is yucky, like the color of the army's uniform.
My name is dark, like the inside of a cave
deep inside the Amazon rainforest,
but is bright at the same time, bright like the color yellow.
My name is plain, like a brown empty box.
My name sounds solid, like a moonstone.
My name tastes like a soup with no flavor,
like a Whopper with no meat, like a playground
with no play structure.
My name is Melvin, just plain Melvin.
It doesn't mean anything in any language.
Melvin, a lost name, lost like the guy
who owns the name, lost in the world
full of worries, loneliness, and sadness.
Melvin, it rhymes with the name of a guy
whom I dislike named Kelvin.
My name is soooo dead
and quiet.

Melvin Cano, 16
International Studies Academy High School

For My Brother

I need to write
about my brother.
He is locked up,
away from his family,
lonely and depressed,
trying his best
to get out.
Without a doubt,
holding his pain inside.

I miss my dad.
I wish my life would pass.
I feel like a mother filled with comfort.
I feel like he will be OK,
just hold on and pray.
I guess I am just worried,
worried for Anthony,
alone in there dealing with his pain.

*Thinking is life worth
living? Should I blast myself?*

I worry about him,
trying hard to be there for him.
I am only 16,
I have my own dreams.
I want to go to college,
I want to get good pay,
no more struggles.
That's the way I want it to be,
taking care of my family.
I need to write for Anthony.
I feel his pain when he says
being incarcerated is driving him insane.

Antoinette Talavera, 16
International Studies Academy High School

P.A.S.E. / MLK After School Lab

Misinformed

That's right, boy,
I'm throwing it in your face:
Us Latinos, we're all the same race.
But do understand,
we all come from a different place.
Don't try to diss—
you just mad 'cause
I'm making you hear this.
I bet you're feeling this small
'cause I'm standing this tall.

*I'm getting to you
little girl,* you say?
No, no, I'm a woman.
Don't let my angel eyes
and vicious thighs fool you.
'Cause, baby, do me wrong
and this Salvadorian warrior
will cut right through you,
all up in my grill
talking 'bout I'm real.
Ha, ha, ha, boy, you better recognize,
always calling me Mexican,
always judging me 'cause of my skin,
sweetheart, you don't know where I've been.

Let me explain:
years of civil war / running / exhausted
frightened / exasperated.
I don't want to die,
I need to be alive.
Let me take you through the time

when my people were mimes / they were ignored.
I've been through poverty / hunger / misery
images of hell / nightmares / black sorrow
the sacrifice for a better tomorrow.

I've seen through the eyes of a blood-drenched child
who comes home to find his mother
lifeless upon the dirt-covered ground,
and a letter from his father
bidding farewell
because he was taken
for being a poor farmer,
they used him as a bulletproof vest.

I ain't trying to hate
all you Mexicans out there.
Damn, y'all quite a race!
We should keep struggling,
we'll get there someday.

I need to fight to be heard,
need to fight for my Salvadorian pride.
We have walked on burning soil
so we need to unite / stop trying to hide.
I know we small,
but we need to shout.
That's right,
I'm throwing it in your face:
Us Latinos, we're all the same race,
but do understand,
we all come from a different place.

Wendy Soriano, 16
International Studies Academy High School

Newcomer High School

Dear Diary

My Dear Diary,
You are my mind.
You keep my deep secrets in white
pages with black or any kind of color.
I use you to write my sadness, happiness,
my tears, my happy faces, my secrets.
You know my handwriting! If it is neat
and clear, you know that I'm happy.
If my handwriting is unclear and
I use slang words, you know how horrible I am,
maybe with tears, with sad face.

You are a simple notebook made of paper,
some pictures, some color ink, but with
millions of thoughts. You know how
mischievous I am. You know how defective
I am because you know my body,
my face, how I am physically.
How honest I am—you know everything about me!

You have letters with powerful meanings.
I get my willpower from you
because on you I discharge my pain
for being alive, because someone hurt me,
or sometimes just my positive things.

Thank you, my Diary! Thank you for being
the other part of my mind and myself.

Laura Melgarejo, 17
International Studies Academy High School

Everywhere

I love you while I'm swimming.
I'm imagining you're a swimming pool, so I dive deep
in your clean water. I can feel you on every single
centimeter of my skin.
I can smell your rose perfume while I'm breathing.
I'm getting out of the pool and now
you're my towel, sliding over my whole body smoothly.
I'm going home now, and you're the jacket that makes me warm.
Finally I get home and when I open the door, I see you
there, so I don't need the jacket or even the towel to dry
my body. Now I feel your skin on my skin, and we make
ourselves warm in my bed.

Julia Pinheiro, 17
Newcomer High School

I Shine

Inspired by Maya Angelou's "Still I Rise"

You may tell people in your neighborhood your bitter, twisted lies.
You may hate me until my dying day, but still like the sun I shine.
You may not like me 'cause the color of my eyes.
You may feel a little tension, but even on rainy days I shine.

You may talk about me behind my back and even make jokes.
You may think I'm dumb or very ghetto, but still like the sun I shine.
You may think I'm not a balla or even call me broke.
You may call me every name in the book, but still like the sun I shine.

You may say little things or do little things or even call me bitch.
You may say I'm scary and not gonna do nothing, but you really know I hits.
You may try to play hardball, but don't know who's going to take the first pitch.
You may try to wear some too big shoe, but you can't if it don't fit.

As I said before, I know you know I got some beautiful eyes.
You may try your hardest to put out my fire, but still like the sun I shine.

I shine, I shine, I shine
Please don't hate.

Kim White, 17
Mission High School

My Favorite Object Is a Pencil

It is nice to have a pencil.
My favorite pencil
has two different colors.
One is black and the other is blue,
which represents me.
My pencil is 2 inches wide and 12 centimeters long
with 0.5 lead.
It helps me write very well and makes me feel happy
every time I write with it.
My lucky pencil keeps me going,
keeps me smart.
Every time I look at it, I see my self,
black as in my mirror, pencil that
reminds me who I am in life.

Nyuma Weah-Weah, 17
International Studies Academy High School

Who Am I?

I am a woman from the west
and there is no best.
I take my time to make a decision
and never settle for less.
I lead my own life
'cause I am no one's wife.
I live life day by day
'cause there is no other way.
Am Amber,
Black queen is what I am.

Think of me as a genius
in my own little way.
Think of me as an activist
because I always have something to say.
Think of me as an athlete,
you know I could do it all
when it comes to every sport,
but I really enjoy softball.
Think of me as an individual
because I can only be me.
But what's most important
is to think of me as Amber
or Shorty, if you really know me.

Don't think of me as ghetto
just because that's where I'm from.
Don't think of me as an immigrant
because my people were forced to come.
Don't think of me as a child
because I am not 18 yet.
Don't think of me as ignorant
because I don't know what something means.

I am Amber Shanta Bacchus,
that's who I am for real.
I'm 5'2" with brown eyes
and, no, I don't steal.
I am here to live a meaningful life,
have four children and be someone's wife.
I am me and that's for real.

Amber Bacchus, 17
Mission High School

No

Every time I try to go to a store, I always hear "No."
Or, "No niggers allowed."
Whatever they feel like sayin'
they say it.
Stories of a black,
I tell you they get deeper and deeper every time.

I'm not talkin' from a view I know about,
but a view my Mom down to my ancestors know about.
I'm not sayin' us blacks did nothing wrong,
but I never seen no sign saying,
"No Whites Allowed."

Michelle Ward, 17
Mission High School

Fu*k the Police

I'm not going to put up with the police
pulling me over saying I fit
the description of a suspect of a robbery
that happened 10 minutes ago.
I'm not going to put up with the police
pulling me over just because I drive
a nice car.
I'm not going to put up with the police
searching me for drugs
just 'cause I wear baggy clothes.

Craig Lewis, 17
Mission High School

Freedom

Nothing is worth more than you.
You're four times priceless.
With you in my life I'll always be right.
When I lose you, I go crazy inside and out.
If I had a choice between you
and life forever,
I would choose you.

I know I took you for granted,
but I didn't know your value
until you were gone.
I promised I'd get you back,
and now that I've got you, I know
how to treat you.
Abuse you I will not.
Put you in danger I will not.
You'll be with me forever.

The only thing is,
when I get you, will I forget
the nightmare that made me love you so much?
I know I've done it in the past,
repeatedly, so many times—
that's why you should leave me forever.

But I've learned how to keep you.
People envy you because I treat you
with so much care.
Every day you bring joy to me
beyond the third power.
Words are not enough to express what I feel.

Sometimes I want to ask you,
Why are you so much
a part of my life?

But if I asked and you told,
I would want to know more.

That's why I take you, my Freedom,
to the heart.
You're the only thing
that keeps me out of the dark.
I know we'll not part again.
To know what I know now
is to know that I want
to keep you forever.

Maurice H., 17
Log Cabin Ranch

Mission High School

Dad

If you don't get a job now, then you'll be broke.
You better get on the ball.
You better get a clue.
You can't be up under me like your sister all your life.
Take out the garbage now!
You got any dirty clothes?
I'm gone.
Why can't nobody wash the dishes?
Who ate all the Krispy Kreme glazed doughnuts?
Why can't you just do what the teacher says?
Why do I always gotta come up to this school for this b.s., Taytay?
That's ridiculous.
This don't make no sense.
So what you gonna do?
You better make up your mind.
Clean your room. It looks like a pigsty.
Stop picking on your brother.
Stop throwing the ball in the house.
Where you going?
I know you don't plan on going nowhere.
Believe me, I know.

Dionté Swanson, 17
Mission High School

The Bus to the Big House

It seemed like I grew up in the middle of the night,
because where I'm from there is no light.

I never go nowhere wit'out havin' a fight,
I guess that's because we have unequal rights.

Young homies don't tell me that the light
they shine in our faces is too bright,
because it's easy to see they're tryin'
to put us away for life.

Nowdayz we just doin' anything,
tryin' to earn these stripes,
but we gon' keep thinkin' it's cooh until
they hit us with that third strike.

So before we make that move,
let's take a moment to think twice.
Because they ain't playin' no mo',
they throwin' us in the pen,
especially if we ain't white.

Don't wait fa no bus ta go ta San Quentin,
let's take a vacation,
let's take a flight.
They love seeing us kill each other,
so let's get together
and re-unite.

Leo P., 17
Log Cabin Ranch

Taste My Tears

At night I cry.
Do you care to know why?
Probably because of the demons
that chase me.
The dirt I did is catchin' up,
even I'm startin' to hate me.
Excuse me, I apologize,
because that there is far from true.
I love myself,
but I truly hate the evil things I do.
At night I cry.
Neglected, abused, and misdirected—
is that pain an excuse?
Could you forgive, forget, live happily-ever-after
if I did those things to you?
I wonder,
and at night I cry.
I started off with good intentions.
In the beginning I had big dreams.
Now I'm surrounded by these green fiends,
and it seems everybody ignores my pleas
for help.
My mama told me, "Be strong and help yourself,"
but what can you do
when your demented mind is detrimental
to your own health?
Not a damn thang except get high,
keep it all inside 'cause you too numb to cry,
except when it's late at nighttime.
In the meantime, I'm just waitin' to die,
3:30 in the morning, talkin' to the walls
'cause I can't sleep.

Wishin' for a phone call.
Damn y'all,
it's hard for me to deal with me.
Yeah it's hard for me to deal with me.
I ain't gone perp.
I do exactly what I was told.
When I'm scared, I go to church,
but the voices in my head still be
putting in overtime work.
That's why I'm here now,
and they still tell me to do mo' dirt.
But I rather die first
'cause this hurts, and it can get worse.
But I gotta keep it real.
I couldn't handle that.
I cry at night
waitin' on the walls to talk back.

Joe S., 17
Log Cabin Ranch

Mission Girls

What Do I See When I Look in the Mirror?

What do I see when I look in the mirror?
When I look in the mirror I see a pretty beautiful
Black young woman
with a good and kind heart.
I see me: the person who always keeps a smile
and stays laughin'.

I also see all the good on the outside
and try to forget about the bad on the inside.
The hurt, feeling broken-down, the pain.
Feeling like someone stabbed me in my heart
with a knife.
Sadness. Crying. The tears I shed. Anger.
I see myself as an American flag
with two colors added:
black and purple.
The red stands for anger that's inside.
The black stands for hurt inside.
The blue stands for sadness on the outside
and sometimes inside.
The white stands for shy, quiet,
innocent on the outside, but
the purple stands for laughing, smiling me.
The sometimes happy me.

Tee-Jai Lampkins, 16
The Center for Young Women's Development

My Heart

My heart is a single teardrop
falling down a lonely cheek.
My heart is a bitter statement
that it so much wants to speak.
My heart wants to go to battle,
it's unclear who it needs to fight.
So my heart will be a stalker
watching, waiting in the night.

Tashiana Jefferson, 16
International Studies Academy High School

Book

Page by page, dark printed words glow out of that white page.
Day by day, the hard covers weaken as the users use them.
Read by night and day, like gawking and mesmerize.
The book has its life and boredom by its shelves,
waiting to be read, sharing its story.
The book only becomes too real when a reader reads it.
Maybe it's time not to judge the book by its cover
because it is time to share and to tell
what we have in common with the story.
Or maybe we too are characters in this world,
like everyone has its script,
like "the world is a stage."
Maybe we don't live long,
but a book can always be saved for the future, or live long
enough that it can be rewritten for the benefit of those generations
and still feel, hear, smell, think
what was it like before then.

Vicente Nalam, 16
International Studies Academy High School

How You Figure?

Inspired by Horace Coleman's "Poem for a 'Divorced' Daughter"

If some nosey body asks, "Where are you from?"
Tell them, "Does it matter where I am from?"

If that ain't enough and they ask again,
Say, "Why you care?"

And if they still want to know,
Tell them, "I am from where you're from."

And if they say, "No you ain't,"
Tell them, "How you figure?"

Anna Vongvixay, 16
International Studies Academy High School

Mission High School

Invisible

I am a single name.
I am one in six billion.
I am the least important person
in everyone else's world.
I am the black sheep of the human race.
I am a depressed poet.
I am that knife slicing my own neck.
I am that kid who can't care about anything
because no one cared about him.
I am that guy who got shot
for stepping on someone else's shoes.
I am that boy who got robbed
because he stepped in the wrong neighborhood.
I am that gun you cock back
when it comes time to handle your business.
I am that drunk father who beats
on his wife and kids
'cause he ain't got nothing better to do.
I am that brother who had to beat up that guy
for slapping his sister.
I am that same curse
that walks the earth unnoticed.

Melvin Jones, 17
Mission High School

The Black Flower

Everywhere I go
I never see a black flower.
I've walked all over the world,
I've never seen a black flower.
I've looked all over the garden,
I've never seen a black flower.
I've asked everyone,
they've never seen a black flower.
I travel country to country,
I never see a black flower.
I ask the olive trees,
they've never seen a black flower.
I ask all the flowers,
they've never seen a black flower.
I ask red, pink, rose, yellow, purple, green,
they've never seen a black flower.
I go back home looking at the mirror
and I ask myself,
Are you the black flower?

Emmanuela Ocean, 18
International Studies Academy High School

Mercy Services

Dragon in Eagle's House

I am Chinese living in the United States.
Chinese is the offspring of dragon.
I am the offspring of dragon.
Dragon means powerful and elitist.
I have no power in the U.S.
Eagle is more powerful than dragon
because this is eagle's house.
Eagle doesn't treat dragon well
because dragon is going to grab eagle's food.
But dragon won't grab eagle's food.
Dragon will help the eagle build its land.

Fu Xiong Zeng, 19
International Studies Academy High School

Leaving Mexico, Coming to America

I am in Mexico group old year two.
I deaf. Hear not, and school people deaf.
I grow up birthday old 15 year.
My mom talk sign not. I sign or deaf hear sign.
I fine sad sign, my mother like not sign.
I school friends deaf same girl.
My friends miss, by Mexico fly.
I sad miss bye.
My mother look wrong, why I cry friends.
My mother side America want I not no.
I escape America with mom escape.
I scared police America.
I America look pretty, fun.
I school deaf new different sign.

Rocio Gonzalez Zuniga, 19
English Literacy, Deaf Education Program
International Studies Academy High School

True Identity

Why do so many people ask me where I come from?
I was born in America, and my parents came from China.

Why do so many people tell me that I am not a real Chinese?
I have yellow skin, black eyes, and black hair.

Why do so many people tell me to go back to China?
I was brought up in America, and I am a legal U.S. citizen.

Why do so many people consider me a foreigner?
I attend school here, and I can read, write, and speak English fluently.

Why do so many people not know my true identity?
I can tell them proudly that I am an American Born Chinese.

Nicholas Lei, 18
International Studies Academy High School

Think Twice

Someone has stolen my crown,
stuck a knife in my heart
and turned me upside down.
Tied me to the ceiling,
and now I'm eternally bleeding.
Rolled the dice
for my life
and didn't even
think twice.

Marlon R., 19
Log Cabin Ranch

San Francisco Public Library, Main Branch

When You Call My Name

My Vietnamese name is Ngoc Lien.
My mom says it is a precious stone.
When my teacher says my name
it sounds like she is angry with me about grades.

My Mandarin name is Yu Len.
It sounds so sweet
when my friends call me.
It sounds like, "Come here, I'll give you some candy."

My Cantonese name is Yoc Lien.
It's a kind of flower that grows in lakes with pink color.
When my parents call me
it sounds like, "You have to stay home to do your work."

My English name is Jane.
It sounds like something very strange to me.
When Manh calls, my name is "DE."
In Vietnamese it sounds like "lustful,"
so I usually hit him.

Jane Dang, 18
Newcomer High School

Slashed in Two

I am an immigrant in America.
Slashes are in my body.
Immigration tears me apart.
Half of me is left in China.
In my dreams, I am walking in my hometown.
In the days, I am studying in my school.

William Huang, 18
International Studies Academy High School

Maria, Who?

Maria, my sister who I wish
every day was still here.
Where have you gone?
And why did you have to leave so soon?
Maria, who?
The mother of two
who still need you.
I remember the last day
I seen you.
You were on your way
out to a party.
I remember making it a point
to say bye.
Was it my subconscious?
Who knows.
I remember getting the call.
Me, I got it.
She wanted to talk to Mom or Dad,
didn't want to talk to me.
I made her.
She told me
you were in an accident.
But were you all right?
was all I kept repeating.
With the coldest sounding voice
she said, "No."
I knew you were gone.
I could no longer see straight.
All I could do was cry, cry, and cry.

Sarah Castro, 20
Mission Girls

Who We Are

We are products of one creator,
one race of people
who have been divided by evil.
Evil started by greed, rape, and slavery,
and ended in the genocide of our people,
destroying us slowly
by taking our god, our land, our culture
and our language,
creating generations of oppressed people
who will one day stand together again.
And when we stand together
to reclaim what has been stolen,
there will be no more racism,
no more violence,
no more oppression.

Marlene Sanchez, 21
The Center for Young Women's Development

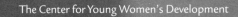
The Center for Young Women's Development

Immigration

We leave a home country,
transfer to a different one.
To make a better future.
To get more money.
To learn about other customs and habits.
To communicate with both tongues.

Immigration is hard.
People cannot imagine.
Different language prevents communication.
Different culture produces an obstacle.
Immigrants always represent low-income, cheap house.
Be careful to manage every cent.
Keep family economy stable.
Working at McDonald's, building houses makes immigrants tired,
need to take a break.

Stand up, newcomer people.
Make your dreams come true.
Use your strong will
to make up for the disadvantages.
Be brave, get in touch with people.
Learn, study everything you don't know.
Be confident. Be patient.

Trust yourself—you have the ability to make
dreams come true.

Steffie Li, 18
International Studies Academy High School

Asian Struggles

Like a bungee, bounce back.
Old-timers with hunch back,
raise your arms and shout, "Bansai," like
delicate branches of bonsai,
twisted twigs, trimmed—toki doki
occasionally, sometimes
we outgrow your restrictions, we stretch
the soil; surpass your limitation.
We might spoil, if we don't uncoil...
We emerge like old food wrapped in foil.

Lives toiled, twigs, our ties,
cuz we stick together
our roots push and pull YOUR theory—
the ground bent over—
hands that prune trees
have freed me.
We dig your holes, which control
and divide our species.
Mama speaks of wan wan
wanton contractors—like Oshiti's.
Can tell lies, exposed, nose grows,
memories, your greed a stampede
that won't heed to your beatings.

And the soles of our traveling,
marching, arched feet
backs of burdens...
The heat boils,
our hearts beat,
and the bubbles and our troubles
will become yours.
Because my "Bansai"
will push your lies out of the way.
And the day will come because
my roots have just begun.
My roots have just begun.
My roots have just begun.

Marjon Kashani, 22
The Center for Young Women's Development

Mission High School

I'll Be Back

Ay, regreso!
was the sentence he often used
after kissing my mom and me good-bye.
Every day it was the same.
The night would pass
and my day would end.
It was as if he were a ghost
who only appeared every blue moon.
He would work all day
and go out at night.
Then finally came the day
when he started to spend
more time at home.
To this day
I just remember him
like an old song.
It's like singing along to a song
you can't remember,
humming and blurting
out a word or two
that you can recall.
Ay, regreso!
was the last thing
that I heard from him.
Pero nunca regresó.

Ingrid Garcia, 18
Loco Bloco

Five-Minute Phone Calls

I need to change my ways
so I don't wind up on the front page,
another intelligent brother that died at a young age.
That's not my destiny
because I feel life has planned something better for me
than beggin' to pee.
And I bet you will see
that I can live life to the best it can be,
just as long as I can believe
that I can achieve
in a world that wasn't made for me.
Just as long as I try and don't act too lazily,
even though the world acts so shadily,
it ain't fazing me!
Trapped in my own emotional rage
and the cage is me,
I hope that I can change before it's too late to see
the light that was made to exceed.
And most of y'all can relate to me when I say,
times these days ain't so easy.
I'm praying that the judge will release me,
five-minute phone calls that just tease me,
wondering when my Momma gonna come see me.
I'm missing her love for sheazy,
and times these days ain't so easy.
So believe me
when I say that hustlin' ain't a pastime,
it's a state of mind,
a way to survive,
and these are the days of our lives.

Stuck in a pit of despair,
heartbroken folks that's committed to theirs,
whether it means hitting a lick
or flipping a kick,
we just trying to get by.
'Cause in the game you ain't meant to get rich
with the system the pimp
and you as the trick.
Who playing who for the grip?
But I ain't condonin' hooligan trips,
like run up on a fool and get split.
Just use this as a tip:
The game is cold and shady,
but maybe
if you said, "Lord, save me,"
took care of your lady or baby,
and put away the 380,
things could get gravy.
In the meantime, do what you can
'cause I understand that
times these days ain't so easy.
I'm praying that the judge will release me,
five-minute phone calls that just tease me,
wondering when my Momma gonna come see me.
I'm missing her love for sheazy.

Daniel T., 18
Log Cabin Ranch

Shadow of Lipstick

The only lights you see
when you come through my block
are the streetlights,
and you hear no voices, just sirens.
Shadow coming from around the corner building.
I remember when I used to go
through my mom's purse
and find nothing but a lipstick
and medicine for her sickness.
From then on, I was at the peak of my mind,
and rose like the September morning sky.

Ben A., 19
Log Cabin Ranch

Girls After School Academy

Earth, No Sun

The breeze of your voice
calmed my earth within.
Beams of your sun
helped me grow with no end.

But when it rained
your sun was covered
with an ugly gray cloud,
the breeze became a strong wind
blowing everything down.

When the rain stopped
my earth was left wet,
cold, and lonely

and still I wait for a sun to hold me.

Jeremiah M., 19
Log Cabin Ranch

Newcomer High School

Rain

How magical favorite nature / falls in the small
drops from clouds in the sky.
It's so beautiful.
I feel comfortable and romantic / when I walk
in the raining day without any umbrella.
It's like my grandmother's hands touch me / when
it falls on my face and hands.
It looks like a wonderful dancer / when it falls
on the leaves of the trees and the ground.
It listens like a great love song / when it falls
on the iron roofs like the beating of drums.
It's rain!

Minny Wang, 18
International Studies Academy High School

5

Poetry Teacher

Poetry arrives on a rusty bike
squeaking across the last bridge to home—and
if the bridge is swept away in April floods
poetry swims across the muddy water
swirling with branches and shoes.

It makes unexpectedly
of the plastic scraps
clutched in a crow's beak,
of the pearls of rain on a flattened ball,
of love, shock, and everything
fallen—poetry
fashions a nest.

It stumbles toward us in the hallways
of sleep, leaving green fingerprints
like moss on the windows.
It arrives by crayon,
by skateboard,
through invisible owls which fly by day.

As they write
I watch their faces for a sign,
for the strange fire to whirl
into the dome of their silence.
I cannot predict when or how
each student will seize hold
those threads of memory and meaning
to weave a coat against the cold—but
that it happens without fail
in each of them,
and poetry takes their hand.

Not right to call myself *poetry teacher*.
I am no conductor, no magician:
The lightning chooses its own moment to speak,
the lotus flower its hour to open,
and poetry beckons in light and leaf
with ragged sandals and machete
to harvest the sugarcane.

We often speak of poetry this way, as visitor,
as spirit that enters
and leaves
our house.
But the children have taught me otherwise—
poetry lives in us always and is not apart.
It is the awakening
to that homeland
where the moonrise casts the grass in platinum
and the wind is alive with voices
answering *yes*

answering
yes and *yes* and *yes*.

Chad Sweeney
Everett Middle School
Mercy Services

A Survey of My Students

The one who wants to be a dragon
  The one who uses "creamy as a lotus petal" in every poem
    The one who searches his pocket dictionary
      for words like "hearty" and "cattail" and "broth"

The one who stormed out
  The one who made me lock the bathroom door and cry
      The one who sang Russian ballads on my acoustic guitar

The one who dreams of being an astronaut,
  The one who works double shifts at Burger King
      The one whose mother still lives in Guangdong
        The one who wrote, "I wish Ishle was my mother"

The one who slept through every class
  then finally! woke up and wrote a poem
    The one I cannot save
        The ones who save me daily

The one who lives with 16 others in a one-bedroom on Valencia
    The one who only talks to me in Spanish
        The one who e-mails me love poems

The one who never opens her mouth
    The one who covers her stomach with a JanSport
        The one whose name I will surely forget
            The one whose eyes I will always remember

The one who draws sketches of dew-wet roses
    The one who folds all his poems in half

The one I cannot save
    The ones who save me daily

Ishle Yi Park
Newcomer High School
San Francisco Community School

Blueprints

The seventh-graders are learning
about anatomy
in the hall.
For an entire October of fourth periods
they are outside room 223
drawing their skeletons
on sheets of butcher paper:
metatarsal, tibia, vertebrae.
I envy science
its textbooks and diagrams,
the certainty of bone.
I teach poetry,
offer 50 minutes
once a week
to write
the frayed edges
of our lives.
The heart is our blueprint,
but the heart
is an unreliable reference;
it will remember a quarter moon
when there was only a muted porch light.
Still, I tell them, be still,
listen:
The heart will tell you a truth
stronger than bone.

Michelle Matz
Everett Middle School

San Francisco Community School

Xin Rong in Four Years

I.
Who are you?
What's your name?
I don't want to do this.
I don't like writing.
I don't like you.
No.
Miss Chávez, do I have to?

II.
You're in this class?
Where's Miss Chávez?
Did she move to Los Angeles?
I'm not going to do it.
I told you no.
No.
There, that's all.
Where's Miss Zamboldi?
Tell her I have a joke.

III.
You're in this class?
If you talk to Miss Chávez,
tell her I said hi.
How do you spell...?
Don't look.
I'm not finished.
Is that right?
Don't show anyone.
There, take it.
Why did you put it
in the book last year?
It was a joke.
I have another one.
Want to hear it?
It's not about you.

IV.
You're in this class?
Want to hear a joke?
Can I have a picture of you?
Did you bring it today?
Did you bring it today?
Did you bring it today?
Don't forget tomorrow.
You brought it?
Look at you standing there
in front of a bus!
You can't be late
for Chinese New Year.
Everybody has to eat
together
sitting down.
I got two envelopes.
Read this.
Miss, read this.
It's in English.
That's Mandarin
not Cantonese.
There's the English.
Read it.
No, you.
I'm not going to.
I read it to myself already.
There's the English.
Did you read it?

If you want to hear it
in Mandarin,
there are those things
to help you.
I'm not going to read it
out loud.
Do you like it?
It's nice, huh?
On the Internet.
I'll show you.
See?

Cathy Arellano
Mission High School
Mission Girls
Loco Bloco

No Canvas, No Gun/Nothing and Everything

Silently swearing
at the streetlights
he shifts his jacket
and checks the gun.
Slow walk; he waits for a man
to show fear, like
his father, and run.
No one comes and he moves to shoot
the lights out.

He catches his breath,
in his hand the metal
changes to
wood, to a thick round brush
now trailing the sky air, the yellow circles
he wanted to blow up and
the weight of his life
pushes back
up
his wrist, the tension even
inside to outside, against this night
the last
that every sorry man was his father.
Just him and this
brush of color over the meter's plastic face up
through his wrist, inside his forehead—watery clear
as colored glass, dripping the concrete walk, a laughing
blood of painters rushes in,
opening the box.

In cobalt now his shadow on the wall, others outlined,
join and flee with purpled bruises. Burnt
sienna words mark, change, kill the abandon
between them. Washed-over ghosts drying
while he walks off the wall, his footsteps printing
escape. In a mirror she inside him is sad
in his hands, made new.
He braids her hair with blue, and turns

on the street
breathing hard.

He ducks from the streetlights wildly hiding
his face from his painting.
It follows him,
it flows in him,
electric.

Where is his gun?

If they could see
him
the world would never
be the same.

Kimberley Nelson
Log Cabin Ranch

A Poem of Thanks to My Students

Slowly they grasp the pen to ignite
thoughts long repressed put in flight,
I want the written word to show me
what the future holds for I and we,
give thanks for this class of students
who learn to be free through poetry.

"I can't imagine that I would be able to
be without language to tell you how I feel"
a seventh-grader scribes on the fly as the pencil
sharpener breaks the silence of a free-write session.
"Take a minute to finish your thoughts," I say,
but they continue to write away.

Take a closer look
search for the poet within
picking up the pen.

Rewrite the text
the seventh generation
we teach to transgress.

Teaching is draining some days, and at times
I feel that no matter all the effort and emotional energy
I invested, I did not make one bit of a difference.
Sometimes I walk out of class feeling drained and defeated.

But then a surprise
"Jime, when you come'n back?"
your hopeful eyes.

I realize
that most change comes gradually,
unexpectedly.

Sometimes we all laugh
sometimes we are all tired
but each day we grow.

Jime Salcedo-Malo
San Francisco Community School

still holding

this year is
dried mango slices from safeway and
popeye's biscuits,
two for ninety-two cents,
when we're studying early in the morning.

this year's a speech that has to get written
for a conference tomorrow,
an essay for an application due today,
a poem that must come together in the next fifteen minutes.

this year
is nachos from the store downstairs
with burnt weak coffee in a styrofoam cup
when class goes way past dinner
and you didn't get lunch.
this year drinks gallons of alka seltzer and licorice root tea
and prays for a calm stomach.

this year has way too much to do
and not enough to do it with and
it's nearly impossible
to pay the bills,
deal with today's news,
and get to work each day.
it's even harder to sit at that table
monday nights and write—
harder still
to convince yourself
someone will listen.

this year needs hershey's kisses by the handful
and those stale red vines you buy five at a time
in a thin brown paper bag.
this year
will eat anything sweet you offer.

this year is a poem
you don't think is any good
but when you finally read it
your voice shakes us awake
made us remember why we brave
the rain and the always-late bus and
all the everyday catastrophes
to get here.

a poem that promises
though you don't know
where you'll stay tonight
you'll be back here tomorrow.
a poem that hopes
enough people show up
to tomorrow's demonstration,
that the officials hiding behind their mahogany rail realize
finally
we matter.
a poem that prays
please don't send our sister
to prison

please let my brother
lying in intensive care
live
please stretch this last dollar
long enough
to get us all home.

a poem about
       how your tired hand still holds that pen
a poem about
       how your throat is raw but your voice still carries
a poem about how your strength
       still holds.

Danielle Montgomery
The Center for Young Women's Development

Our Nature

To advance like an army over the horizon
overtake the fields by day, though our
faces may close tight, soft knots, by night.

Let poetry spread this way, rapidly
opening and disclosing daily in
incessant whispers, in rapid-fire rumbles.

Celebrate, lament, reflect.
Like morning glories let the beauty of our stories
overrun bare fields of hard fact.

Details bound to paper by pen,
to muscle by memory and rhythms
older than the first heart's beat.

Gloria Yamato
Girls After School Academy
San Francisco Public Library, Main Branch
YWCA, Western Addition
Partners in After School Education / Martin Luther King After School Lab

Possibility

Dedicated to the teachers and students at International Studies Academy High School

today i hurried through the hall
amidst a kaleidoscope of color and students
and new poets waiting to be born
just needing a pen and the right to speak

today i hurried down that hall
with bell hooks' mantra running through my head
education as the practice of freedom
and what does this mean
when these poets
who just need the right to speak
face teachers who label them as "gifted"
or "difficult"
and statistics say
some of them will never
make it
or become more
than cracks in the concrete
of this dear city

what does this mean
when these poets
go to school in a state
whose educational system is ranked 41st in the nation
what does this mean
when the same student excuses himself from class
every five minutes
looks me straight in the face and says
this is stupid

even after we spend the day watching "educational"
material like thriller-killer *What Lies Beneath*
instead of *Slam*
they still write
even if the words bleed
pink / yellow / blue
or the latest concoction
of gel pen colors
fingers sweat
typing word after word
eager to finish the final poetry folder

so even in the midst
of backpacks / bullies
and the final bell
even after someone told me
you teach poetry
that can't be so challenging
even after i begin to wonder
if people think poetry teachers
do nothing more than carry rhyming dictionaries
to school

i still hurry
down the hall
i throw out lesson plans
some days
but it doesn't matter
because i come
with my pen
and extra ones
for these new american poets
who just need the right to speak
i pick up my pen
i use my tongue
i search for a raised eyebrow
a hand flying in the air
with any answer
a head tilted in my direction
i come here to fight
for nothing less
than possibility

Uchechi Kalu
International Studies Academy High School